The
Highway Code
for Retirement

Published 2012 by CWR, Waverley Abbey House, Waverley
Lane, Farnham, Surrey GU9 8EP, UK. Registered Charity No.
294387. Registered Limited Company No. 1990308.

Names in this book have been changed to protect identities.

All the quotations are cited in the *International Thesaurus
of Quotations* (London: Penguin Books, 1983).

See back of book for list of National Distributors.

Concept development, editing, design and production by CWR.

Printed in China by C&C Offset Printing Co., Ltd.

ISBN: 978-1-85345-668-8

The Highway Code for Retirement

David Winter

CWR

With his superb gifts of communication, David Winter has given us a splendid guide for retirees, which both those facing retirement and those long retired will find immensely helpful. Comprehensive yet succinct; its contents are summed up in clear checklists; it is positive, practical and challenging, with the warmth of real experience and observation, and it is entirely pervaded with the breath of a mature walk with Christ.

Bishop Michael Baughen

Retirement – many of us dread it but, like death and taxes, it's usually unavoidable. Will it be an idyllic endless holiday or a miserable epilogue to real life? David Winter's book gives us a few tips to help us find a middle way between those extremes, with advice on a variety of topics – from looking at the financial side of it, to coping with resentment at feeling 'over the hill' and looking at life after death. Talking about it in an open and humorous way, it's well worth reading now, whatever stage of life you're at.

Cindy Kent, former singer with the 'Settlers', radio presenter and now Anglican vicar

Contents

Introduction

*Few men of action have been able to make a
graceful exit at the appropriate time*
(Malcolm Muggeridge, *The Twilight of Greatness*)

For once, Malcolm Muggeridge was wrong. In fact,
surveys show that most people – including men and
women of 'action' – do, in fact, enjoy retirement. But
for many of us, including the author of this book, it
doesn't come easily. There seems to be an art of retiring
gracefully or happily – or perhaps it is a skill to be learnt.
The object of this book is to try to identify that art or skill
in the hope that those approaching retirement, or newly
retired, may be saved months or even years of trying to
find it the hard way, by trial and error.

Head in the sand?

Some of you might feel that you are too young to be
interested in reading a book about retirement. But it's a
good idea to be prepared for the changing seasons of life.

In 2011, as I write this, many people either do not
feel 'ready' to retire at 65, or cannot afford to do so. Yet
eventually and inevitably working life will end for almost
all of us, and it is simply hiding our heads in the sand to
pretend otherwise. Sooner or later, it's a change we shall
have to face.

A modern experience

Retirement is a relatively modern experience.
Until the Industrial Revolution, it was fairly unknown.
People went on working on the land, or in a workshop
or market, until they were too old to do it any longer.

Then they surrendered themselves to the care of the extended family, sitting in their favourite chair and giving the younger generation the benefit of their wisdom accumulated over the years. Although, as the average expectation of life was somewhere in the forties, they could consider themselves lucky if they ever made it to that precious armchair. Most people, men and women, 'died in harness' – many women, sadly, in childbirth.

More than a clock

However, over the last 150 years or so, the idea of retirement at the end of one's working life has become accepted. Seventy-two years ago my grandfather retired after a lifetime working for the Great Western Railway, clutching his retirement reward – a rather splendid clock. Modern expectations go a bit further, and so do the hopes and fears we bring to it. Our personality types play a big part in what we might expect life to be like when we retire. Aging is a process, but 'old' is a state of mind.

Aging is a process, but 'old' is a state of mind.

MEMO

Two images of retirement

There are two stereotypical images of retirement. The first is of a kind of idyllic endless holiday – getting up late, pottering in the garden, seeing friends, travelling – in fact, doing all the things you were never able to do during the years of work.

The second is of a grumpy old person, regarded by everyone else as well past their sell-by date, watching daytime television and complaining bitterly about how boring life is. Any attempts to persuade them to action are met by the single abrupt answer, 'I'm too old for that!'

It happens to everyone

Needless to say, neither picture is a fair or accurate image of retirement, though I have to admit I know a few who fit fairly accurately into the second picture. In any case, the choice is ours. We know it's coming. Retirement of the happy vacation or desperately dreary kind is not a state you just slip into accidentally. It's seldom unbroken bliss, or unrelieved tedium. For those of us fortunate enough to be able to retire, what we make of it is up to us.

Happiness – and happiness lost

Many retired people are very happy. For the fortunate among us, if there has been a mortgage, it's probably paid off; any children have (usually!) flown the nest; there is enough money to live on, and a lot more time to enjoy life. But there are at least three sets of 'retirees' for whom that is not the picture at all.

   If many people enjoy their retirement, it raises the question why others don't. There can, of course, be many reasons for this – financial, personal, temperamental and circumstantial. Some people are naturally more able to cope with changing patterns of life. Some distrust any kind of change. Knowing ourselves may help us to see why we feel anxious or even resentful about the prospect of retirement, but to see it as simply another stage of life's journey, with possibilities as well as problems, may help. In this, as in so many things in life, being positive is much, much better than being negative.

   The three sets of retirees who struggle are those who are:

HARD UP
Sadly there are those for whom retirement is a matter of bare financial survival – no money for anything beyond necessities, and a constant struggle to pay the bills. Over 2,000 years ago a Roman writer called Cato

pointed out that 'cessation of work is not accompanied by cessation of expenses'. Nothing changes! That's why we shall be looking at some of the financial questions facing those about to retire. It may not be too late to do something about it.

FED UP
Another group are not particularly poor financially, but they never really take to retirement. Instead of accepting it as a fact of life, they resent the very idea of being retired, and either fight it (and lose) or eventually decide that they are now over the hill and past it, and simply give up.

But retirement does not mean we are 'over the hill'.

MEMO

But retirement does *not* mean we are 'over the hill'. It does *not* mean we are 'past it'. It simply marks a moment when full-time paid employment is no longer the daily shape of our lives. It doesn't mean we've ceased to be the same people we were before, and it doesn't mean we suddenly become valueless or useless.

... AND SCARED!
The third group is those people who have specific fears about being retired. These may be financial, or about status and self-worth (who am I now?), or about the effect it will have on their daily routine. Often these are the kind of people who find it hard to adjust to new circumstances (a pretty common condition!), and correctly regard retirement as something scarily new.

One way to face this kind of fear is to look back at changed circumstances earlier in life: leaving home, for instance, or getting married, or moving to a new job. All of these, too, involved major changes in the scenery of our daily lives, but generally speaking we were able to deal with them. Retirement is probably less drastic a change than most of those. We are likely to stay in the same home (although retirement can mean we have to make a major decision about this) and live with the same people. The change will be to our daily routine, and we shall be thinking about what that means later.

One big change that will eventually follow retirement is, of course, growing old – depending on the age of retirement – with its natural final destination, death.

Fears to be faced

The moment of retirement may well be a time when fears begin to arise about illness, bereavement, old age and death – our own, or that of someone we love. There is a section on this later in the book, but in terms of fears to be faced this obviously needs to be recognised. We shall not have a very happy retirement if it is overshadowed by such terror. On the other hand, facing these issues now will be the best possible preparation for coping with them later. A quiet faith that our lives, and those of the people we love, are in the hands of God will make a huge difference.

My three retirements

This book is written by someone who knows from personal experience a bit about all these responses to retirement. After all, I've done it three times: from my main lifetime's work, from a post-retirement occupation, and then from a part-time job. All of that took place within ten years of compulsory retirement at sixty, which in present terms seems ridiculously early. So I'm not the perfect retiree by any means, and when I write about mistakes and misapprehensions, I do so from bitter experience.

The retired 'homemaker'

Incidentally, when we speak of retirement it's important to remember that there is also a group of people (rarer these days than before) who may never have worked outside the home, or who at least have little experience working in a full-time occupation. They are the homemakers – maybe, for example, those who have dedicated at least part of their lives to bringing up a family. They, too, face a serious life-change at about the same time as the people who leave full-time paid employment. The children have grown up, the 'nest' is empty, the task to which they dedicated the best years of their lives is completed. Now, what do they do? A part-time job might have been interesting, but if that has ended as well life could seem pretty bleak. If it coincides with the retirement of the one who used to be called the 'breadwinner' then there may be a doubling of the anxiety.

Something to look forward to

I appreciate that all of this sounds as though I'm treating retirement as a 'problem' (or in modern jargon a 'challenge'). Well, the insistent theme of this book is that it isn't. Like most worthwhile things, it's not always easy, but most people actually enjoy it, so there's no real reason why you shouldn't, too!

But journeys and pilgrimages are meant to go somewhere, and so is retirement.

MEMO

Part of the journey

What is certainly true is that retirement is something that is better planned for and looked forward to than an event that suddenly overtakes us. Like adolescence, marriage, the arrival of children and grandchildren, and getting older, it's simply a part of the journey of life for most people. We sometimes talk about 'rites of passage' – things such as baptism, leaving school, marriage and so on. Well, retirement is one of those, just a stage on a journey – or, in religious language, a pilgrimage. But journeys and pilgrimages are meant to go somewhere, and so is retirement.

Make the most of the years

At sixty-five the average man has a further fifteen years of life ahead of him, and the average woman, twenty. It would be a pity to waste them, wouldn't it? *Fifteen years is a long while to sit and watch daytime television!* Just look at what some people have achieved as they have got older:

- Winston Churchill became Prime Minister and inspired a nation at war aged sixty-six
- Ronald Reagan became the fortieth President of the USA aged sixty-nine
- Michelangelo was appointed architect for St Peter's in Rome at seventy-four, and was designing churches at eighty-eight
- Nelson Mandela became President of the Republic of South Africa aged seventy-five
- Claude Monet began painting his 'Water Lily' series at seventy-six, and finished the work at eighty-five
- John Glenn flew in space aged seventy-seven
- Mother Teresa was still leading her work among the poor in Calcutta aged eighty-six
- Picasso was still painting at the age of ninety-one

Feeling inspired now? Read on.

Planning for retirement

¾m

planning for the transition; pensions;
supplementing your income; preparing
emotionally and spiritually; Ten Planning
Commandments

65

¾ mile
ahead

Planning for retirement

One cannot rest except after steady practice
(George Ade, *The Man Who Was Going to Retire*)

No one should let retirement sneak up on them. It's definitely best planned for. Indeed, a bit of practice might help! Most of us have some idea when it will happen, either because it's part of our terms of employment, or because we know when whatever paid work we're doing is due to end, whether this is our decision, someone else's or due to circumstances. There are a few simple guidelines about this planning.

MEMO **No one should let retirement sneak up on them.**

Drawing up an agenda for retirement

I know some people who have found it very helpful and positive to draw up a kind of agenda for retirement – 'Things I would like to do, and things I want to avoid'. Make sure you discuss it with your partner, if you have one. It's no good planning a retirement on the Costa Brava if your partner is set on living out their days within ten miles of the grandchildren in Birmingham!

Of course, you may not be free to make these kinds of decision on retirement. You may find that you are needed to look after an elderly parent or babysit grandchildren!

What kind of life do you want?

But the more profound parts of such an agenda are what one might call 'spiritual' goals. What kind of a life would you like to lead? Are there ambitions, goals, that you would love to have the chance to fulfil, given the opportunity? Learning a language, writing your life story, signing up for voluntary work, visiting the Holy Land, taking up a new hobby, finding old friends, picking up old contacts – things like this can make the prospect of retirement seem much more appealing.

For many people, far more important than all of those is asking ourselves what *God* might want of us from those precious years of retirement. This gift of extra time can provide space for prayer and reflection, space which we have missed in the busy-ness of pre-retirement life. Freed from other responsibilities, can we take on new ones, in the church, in the community, or in our own circle of friends and neighbours – a new kind of 'calling' or vocation for our later years?

Christians might feel that retirement offers a precious opportunity to serve God in new ways. Health permitting, age is no barrier. People in their seventies have become Street Pastors, ministering in city centres to vulnerable young people. Others could take on some serious study of the Bible (there are plenty of courses available by correspondence and the Internet), or offer help with short-term church projects – children's holiday weeks, perhaps, or visiting on housing estates. This kind of service in the retirement years can be especially helpful for those who are on their own, giving a sense of purpose and of 'being needed'.

When age or infirmity restrict the ability to get out and about or serve in practical ways, one might develop a whole new kind of service – prayer for others, not just friends and family, but for difficult situations within our own community and the wider world. One of the great things about prayer is that it can span the universe! We are never too old to develop a closer relationship with God, to 'practise the presence of God' even in the routine of daily life, as Brother Lawrence advocated. Simply to list some of these goals for fulfilment in retirement makes it sounds less threatening – indeed, fulfilling and rewarding.

Things you may want to avoid

As for the things we might plan to avoid, each person's list will be different. However, it's worth asking ourselves whether we are happy to be drawn into running things (clubs, groups, courses) or not. Believe me, the invitations will come! The newly retired are rightly seen as a marvellous resource of untapped energy. Look at the people who volunteer to help in local charities and organisations, including the local church. Probably many of them fall into that category. Ask yourself whether you are ready to be approached, and what your response would be.

Fighting mental rust

On my list of things I wanted to avoid was boredom or mental stagnation. I'd kept my brain pretty busy at work. I didn't want it to rust in retirement. Mental exercise is as important as physical – and, as you grow older, probably more important. Some people combat mental rust with a daily crossword puzzle or sudoku, or learning how to surf the Internet! I found regular Bible reading, challenging radio programmes, books, the theatre, an interesting daily newspaper and plenty of conversation were the best remedies for me.

Plan for the transition

For many people, it is the first few months of retirement that are crucial. The sudden change of routine and the instant loss of 'status' can come as a shock if we aren't ready for them. We are constantly defined by our occupation, even in court. 'Samuel Jones, fifty-two, lorry driver' is the typical newspaper summary of a person's status. At social events, in casual conversation people ask, 'What do you do?' – and they don't mean sing under the shower or part your hair on the left.

It's one thing to be able to answer, 'I'm a nurse, or a butcher, or an accountant', and quite another to reply, 'Oh, I'm retired'.

What I used to be

'Retired' seems to imply that you've withdrawn from real life, like the batsman at cricket who 'retires', to play no more part in the match. Personally I quickly learnt to add what I'd retired *from*. 'I used to be a Premier League footballer, a ballerina or lead singer in a boy band' will probably ensure an interesting follow-up conversation.

Change of routine

The loss of perceived status affects some people more than others. After all, many of us never had much 'status'. But the instant change of routine affects everyone on retirement. It's surprising the way our job shapes the pattern of our lives, from the time we wake in the morning to the company and location we share during the eight hours or so of the average working day.

Suddenly, there are people!

Some jobs, of course, are essentially lonely, such as long-distance lorry driving. Those whose work is largely solitary might find the sudden need to relate to family, neighbours and friends all day long quite a trial. That is, of course, the exact opposite of those (the majority) who miss the company of friends and colleagues at work.

The last months at work

Being prepared mentally for these changes helps. Our last months at work can usefully be a kind of 'winding down' period in which we begin to reassess the various demands on our time, the relative importance of work and home, and loosen our dependence on the familiarities of colleagues, setting and daily routine. (Although for many they are busier than ever as they clear up, prepare to hand over, say their goodbyes …) It is helpful to begin to put a few post-retirement dates and events in the diary, things to look forward to. Changes are always best when they are prepared for and anticipated with pleasure rather than anxiety.

A pre-retirement Gap Year?

It's fairly normal nowadays for young people planning to go on from school to university to have a 'Gap Year' – a year when they do something completely different, to build a kind of bridge between the very ordered and prescriptive life of school and the less organised, freer style of university life. It helps them to grow up, to approach the transition between two lifestyles with an acclimatising interval in between.

Quite often one finds people taking a similar 'Gap Year' at the point of retirement. Rather than go straight from working life to the life of the retired, they plan six months or a year doing something completely different. A married couple I know marked his retirement from a job he had done for forty years with six months in South Africa, not going on safari and photographing wild animals, but helping in a community project which they had supported at a distance for many years.

At least when the experience was over they could look forward with renewed enthusiasm to the quieter lifestyle they had associated with retirement but had secretly half dreaded.

Of course, this may not be possible for everyone, depending on age and income bracket. But 'time out' is generally a good idea. For some, planning a retreat or short-term change of scene could prove helpful in the transition period.

Seeing retirement as the 'Sabbath' of life

Many of us are familiar with the Jewish idea of 'Sabbath' – the biblical principle that life consists of a pattern of work, activity and rest. The Sabbath was instituted as a mandatory day of rest every week – one in seven. On that day, even the farm animals were given a break.

The principle of a weekly day of rest from work has been taken into virtually every human culture. In fact, we've expanded it. We look forward to what we call the 'weekend'. Equally, we enjoy the promise of a summer holiday, bank holidays, festivals and feast days, which are features of our social calendar. In a way, these are all expressions of the 'Sabbath' principle.

I've always found it helpful to think of retirement as the 'Sabbath' of life; the evening's rest awaiting us at the end of a lifetime of work and responsibility. The Sabbath isn't just 'not working', however. It's *being* rather than *doing* – and that's the thing that makes retirement something to look forward to rather than to dread. 'Sabbath was made for man,' said Jesus, 'and not man for the Sabbath' (Mark 2:27, NKJV). He didn't see the Sabbath as an irksome restriction, the forbidding of things we would rather be doing, but as a wonderful gift of rest, relaxation and reflection. In the same way, retirement is not meant to be seen as a restriction, a diminishing of our lives, but as an opportunity to live more fully. It's meant to be good, not bad; a blessing, not a handicap.

Don't leave it till it happens

This is particularly true of pension arrangements. If you have lived in the UK for years you have probably been paying National Insurance. It's a good idea to contact The Pension Service and find out your predicted pension on reaching the State Pension Age, which they will be happy to supply. (For those in the UK you can go online to www.direct.gov.uk for that and other helpful information. You will need to tell them your National Insurance number. There will be comparable websites in other countries.) You can then decide whether you're in a position to 'buy' some 'extra years', by making a voluntary contribution to cover periods when for one reason or another you weren't contributing. For some, of course, it will simply not be possible to 'top up' any existing pension, due to current financial issues, but if you can do this it means that your pension will be larger on retirement. You will also find information about the many benefits you are entitled to.

In the same way, it's a good idea to check the exact state of your occupational pension, if you have one. If your company has a Human Resources department, they will be able to give you the current situation – and again you may be able to 'buy' extra years. Sometimes you can have a larger pension later by delaying receiving it – a good idea if you have plans for some other employment or source of income on retirement.

There's usually also the option of taking part of your work pension in a lump sum, with reduced monthly payments subsequently. (Regarding that, it's best to take financial advice.) It's also helpful to know your precise termination date of employment and whether that includes any provision for 'terminal leave'.

Arrange your pension payments

Each country's state pension benefits will operate in a different way, so I am only qualified to comment on the system I know. Obviously you will need to find out what applies within your country.

For UK readers I can offer the following help: Normally The Pension Service will contact you about four months before you reach State Pension Age to make arrangements for State Pension payments, if you are entitled to them. If you don't hear from them three months before reaching that age you can get in touch with them or go online at www.direct.gov.uk and download the State Pension claim form. The payments are paid most simply directly into your bank account, weekly, four-weekly or quarterly, according to your choice – though you can still collect them as cash from the Post Office if you wish.

Your work pension, if you have one (and you may well have more than one from different jobs), will obviously be arranged through your employer, even though it may be provided by an outside agency. Again, it's well to check precisely what the arrangements will be.

Arranging your own pension

If your job doesn't include pension arrangements, then it's wise – but not always financially possible – to make some yourself. There are many personal pension plans and annuities, but you will need to research the possibilities carefully. An Independent Financial Adviser (IFA) is probably the best source of such advice – many will be listed in Yellow Pages or the equivalent, but it's important to distinguish between 'tied' advisers (promoting the services of one or a group of companies) and independent advisers. This distinction is usually made clear in their advertising.

Obviously such schemes are best entered into many years before we expect to retire, but even at the 'last moment' a lump sum invested in a pension 'pot' can provide a useful addition to income in later life. However, not all of us are able to do that. Options such as equity release on property could be considered. This is a very good time to review pensions and savings with a professional advisor.

Supplementing your retirement income

If you think that your income after retirement will be immediately and seriously reduced, you might like to investigate other sources of income that don't involve full-time work but will provide some useful extra money. Of course, this will depend on your age and state of health. Among the jobs that friends and acquaintances of mine have taken on in the early years of retirement are these:

- Newspaper delivery
- Delivering the local 'free' paper
- Dog walking for people who are at work all day
- Light gardening
- Ironing – in great demand!
- Childminding – you need to be aware of the regulations regarding this. You can check the situation with the Child Care Officer at your local council
- Weekend shifts in a supermarket
- Catering for parties, etc
- Private book-keeping/tax returns
- Home tuition
- Music lessons
- Home care work
- Secretary to parish council/local charity
- School lunchtime supervisor

If these options seem rather mundane, you might consider something a little more demanding – you may decide to become a consultant or mentor, sharing your skills and experience with a new generation, or train as a life coach or counsellor.

Remember, if you earn extra income, you need to keep careful note of the sums you receive, and any expenses you incur, in case it affects your tax position. You may even need to register as self-employed – check with HMRC. You might also contact the Tax Office to ensure that you receive the right tax-free allowance, that you are paying the right amount of tax, and so on.

Prepare emotionally and spiritually

As well as these practical arrangements, planning for retirement should involve mental and spiritual preparation. Many larger firms run pre-retirement courses, which in ideal cases include the emotional, psychological and spiritual effects of moving out of work into a radically different lifestyle. Sometimes, however, they simply deal with the practical implication of this change of life, which means that you will need to look for that kind of advice elsewhere. Your local adult education project may run pre-retirement courses, and it's well worth booking a place on one if you can. Books and courses will offer limited help.

For those who believe that their lives are in the hands of God, planning for retirement must surely involve asking what He expects of us in this new phase of our lives. After all, we shall have more time and less daily responsibilities. We may have always wished, for instance, that we had more time to pray, or opportunity to go on retreat or a 'quiet day' somewhere. Well, suddenly we have!

Remember, though, that no two people are exactly the same. What works for one may not work for all.

MEMO

Again, there may be areas of service that we have felt unable to take on because of work commitments. Simply to bring such issues into our thinking and our prayers will open the possibility of a new call on our Christian commitment. To ask God what He wants us to do with our time is a first step. The answer might surprise us.

At a human level, it can help to talk with people who have experienced retirement (choose those who seem to have made a good fist of it!), and draw on their experience. Remember, though, that no two people are exactly the same. What works for one may not work for all.

The last section of this book deals with some of the emotional, psychological and spiritual questions that sometimes arise with retirement – or, perhaps, arise with aging, when we feel less able to cope with our situation.

Ten Planning Commandments for Retirement

1. Plan for it.

2. Check your pensions.

3. Think about a part-time job, or retraining.

4. Consider a pre-retirement course.

5. Consider the lifestyle in retirement that is right for you and for your loved ones – using the extra time given to you responsibly and prayerfully; spend some quality time seeking God for His leading at the start of your new life.

6. List the things to avoid.

7. Fight mental and spiritual rust.

8. Plan for the transition.

9. Consider a Gap Year (or 'time out').

10. Use the last months of work to 'wind down', not get 'wound up'.

Life without work

¹2m

terminus or junction; what will I miss about work; what will I not miss about work; not the end of the journey; Ten Commandments of Life Without Work

Life without work

We combat obstacles in order to get repose, and when got, the repose is insupportable
(Henry Adams)

You'll wake up one cold winter morning with the usual feeling of reluctance to tear yourself from the warm bed – and then realise that you don't have to. You're retired. You can get up when you like, have a leisurely breakfast, read the paper, and then wander to the shops or chat with a neighbour until it's time for lunch. What bliss! It's just like being on holiday …

Terminus, or junction?

But of course this *isn't* a holiday. Holidays end, and normal service is resumed. Retirement, however appealing in prospect, is a major life change. This is how it's going to be from now on. Thinking negatively, it's the terminus. More positively, however, it's more like a junction. One successful change, and the journey is resumed, but on a different train and along different lines.

… it is God's gift that all should eat and drink and take pleasure in all their toil.
(Ecclesiastes 3:13–14, NRSV)

Work, in one sense of the word, is an essential part of being human. From childhood to old age, life involves various forms of work – homework during schooldays, household chores, shopping, doing the washing, gardening, cleaning the car, oiling the bike and so on. We 'occupy' ourselves, because we are active creatures. In the Genesis creation story in the Bible, Adam in the

Garden of Eden – that idyllic setting of perfection – was given work to do: he was put in the garden to 'work it and take care of it' (Genesis 2:15).

Our pet dog or cat is content, left to themselves, to snooze away all day, waking just for meals prepared by someone else (and the occasional foray into the outside world – if it's not raining). Such a lifestyle would strike us as obscenely indulgent, not to say totally boring. Most of us don't like being confined to bed, we hate enforced inactivity, we enjoy 'doing things'. And work is one of the things we do.

But 'work' doesn't end when they stop paying you for it.

MEMO

However, the word 'work' has become attached to only one part of that activity. When we're asked what 'work' we do, we don't answer 'make the fire' or 'weed the garden', but automatically turn to that activity for which we are paid. 'Work', in this definition, is paid employment.

But 'work' doesn't end when they stop paying you for it. When we speak of 'life after work' – meaning when our 'job' comes to an end – we need to recognise that fact. Retirement from daily work doesn't mean an end to activity, or even productivity. We are still active creatures, and while health and strength remain we shall find plenty of things to do. I've lost count of the number of retired people who have said to me, 'I don't know how I ever found the time to go to work.'

What will I miss about work?

Despite that, most people will miss some things about the daily life of work. Those who have not suffered prolonged periods of unemployment, sickness, redundancy, or have taken time out to raise a family, may have had the same pattern of life for forty years or more.

There's the loss of DAILY ROUTINE. In some ways, work will have tended to shape the whole of one's life: the set hours and shifts; leaving home, probably in the morning; the journey to the place of employment; the tea breaks and lunch hours; the end of the working day and returning to the welcome (or indeed the pressures) of home life.

There's the loss of our WORK COLLEAGUES – the ones we liked, and even the ones we didn't. They were the human background to the working day – the familiar faces and voices, the greetings and jokes and odd remarks, the inevitable workplace comedian and the equally inevitable workplace whinger: all part of 'life's rich pattern'.

Most of us like proximity to other people and enjoy social interaction and chat. We don't appreciate isolation or loneliness. Probably among our workmates will be some who are real friends, and we shall miss seeing them every working day.

There's also the SATISFACTION OF WORK WELL DONE. That comes in many guises, of course, largely depending on the kind of work we do. But we all know the feeling when we've successfully completed a demanding task, whether it's serving lunch to 200 primary school children, seeing the last patient, finishing an article for a newspaper or magazine, or balancing the books at the end of the day in the shop or office.

Then there's the question of STATUS, which we mentioned earlier. A job helps to define us, to provide us with a recognisable role in society. In the great kaleidoscope of life, we are 'somebody'. Many of the surnames with which we are familiar relate to the jobs our ancestors did long ago – Smith, Baker, Gardner, Brewer, Thatcher, Butcher, Painter, Groome, Tiler and so on. They were identified – indeed, named – by the work they did, and so, in a way, are we today.

And then of course there's the little matter of PAY. Most of us like to feel that we have earned our keep (as well as needing to pay the bills!), and the regular income of a job gives us the feeling that we have paid our way. Most of us would, on the whole, rather be independent than dependent, and that weekly or monthly payment gives us a feeling of personal value.

What will I not miss about work?

In one way, it's easier to think of what we shall *not* miss about work: the cold mornings waiting for the bus or train, or scraping the ice off the car. We won't miss the pressure to achieve goals and meet targets. We won't miss the anxiety of failure, when a task we have been assigned seems too difficult, too complicated or too demanding for us to cope with.

And some of us will not miss what seems to us the dead hand of routine: the same faces, the same work, even the same jokes. There may also be someone – a boss or a senior colleague, perhaps – whose presence and attitude we shall definitely be pleased to escape from.

It is really important to see retirement as a junction rather than a terminus.

MEMO

Not the end of the journey

It is really important to see retirement (as I've already suggested) as a junction rather than a terminus. It's emphatically *not* the end of life's journey, but it is a junction where we change 'trains'. Life after retirement can't help being different, but it really is the same life, the life God gave us, the life we've known through childhood and all the years since then. We are still the same people: all that has changed is part of the scenery. Hopefully, family, partner, friends are the same. Home is the same (unless we decide to move house). Our interests and concerns are the same. Yes, a big part of our life's routine has changed, but we are not slaves to routine, are we?

Where are we going?

Retirement is the moment when we can ask who we really are, what our goals and interests are, who the people who matter most to us are. Put like that, most of us would have to say that our life of work was only a part of the scenery, not the substance of who we are (although 'workaholics' will struggle more with this issue, and may need to examine what gap work has been filling in their emotional lives; and those who have had a true vocation, and may never have married because of it, may also find it difficult to make the transition). The future can be full of exciting possibilities. The biggest problem facing many of us is not what lies ahead, but a preoccupation with what lies behind!

Ten Commandments for Life Without Work (10)

1. Relax – it's only one of life's junctions.
2. Create a new routine for life.
3. Find new friends.
4. Consider ways to supplement your income (if needed).
5. Find new things to do well.
6. Take on a voluntary job, ministry or service.
7. Cultivate a new interest. Be open to people, circumstances and the quiet voice of the Spirit.
8. Ask yourself what the God who made you and loves you has in store for you now.
9. Set yourself goals – reading, walking, visiting, praying.
10. Be grateful for the extra time.

The others involved

$\frac{1}{2}$m

a new routine; Ten Commandments for the House Invader; making new friends; children; talking it through; the single person

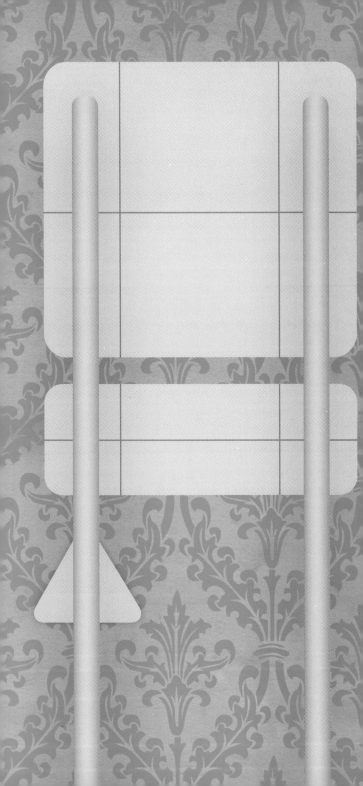

The others involved

Friendship requires more time than poor busy men can usually command
(Ralph Waldo Emerson, *The Conduct of Life*)

Obviously my retirement affects many people beyond just me. A husband or wife will be most closely involved, of course, but the rest of the family, children, grandchildren and friends will to a greater or lesser degree find their lives affected.

MEMO

Our relationships will subtly change when time is no longer a problem but a possibility.

It's equally true for those who are single or widowed at the time of retirement. We will have friends who are very dear to us. Now we have more time for them. We can make contact, arrange to see them, rebuild relationships that are precious to us. We may have nephews and nieces, godchildren, or brothers and sisters whom we have only seen infrequently during the years when work occupied so much of our time. Our relationships will subtly change when time is no longer a problem but a possibility.

If I am married or in a long-term partnership, I shall obviously be 'around' more (for better or worse!), not disappearing for hours on end to that mysterious thing called 'work'. I'll be free to share in events and activities during the working week – and, like it or not, I'll be available to help out with domestic responsibilities, from walking the dog to minding grandchildren and doing the shopping.

It is a 'life partner' that will certainly notice the difference in lifestyle. The partner who ran the home – traditionally the wife – will suddenly find her domain invaded by another person. If she has been a full-time homemaker, instead of seeing her partner off to work in the morning, for example, and then having the house to herself, her husband will be there, sitting in his armchair, fiddling with things, even watching daytime television (which might have been her peculiar privilege, in between the chores). It may seem a trivial difference, but it's a deeply loving partnership that can absorb this particular change without a few tensions.

Adjustments will be called for on both sides. New boundaries may need to be drawn, 'codes of conduct' discussed. For those who share a faith, this is a wonderful opportunity for shared prayer – for tolerance, for the wisdom and grace to accept the change and enjoy it. One of the pleasures of retirement for me was that my wife and I could enjoy the luxury of sharing Bible reading and prayer together every morning.

... the home will need a new routine.

MEMO

A new routine

Apart from anything else, the home will need a new routine. When is coffee time? Do we have biscuits? What about lunch? Do we sit down to it, have it on our laps, or even sometimes go out for a snack? Will some of the household jobs now change hands? What about the bins, the vacuum cleaning, the weekly shop? Changes of this kind aren't what people call 'deal-breakers', but they do need to be faced and answered. Personally, I found shopping together was quite fun – I pushed and carried (and paid at the till) and she chose. Simple!

But you won't do everything together. The male might not fancy 'window shopping', and the female may draw the line at watching rugby. But even decisions of that kind have consequences – decisions that will require give and take. It sounds easy, until you're the one 'giving' and your partner is the one 'taking'! Just wait until you both want to use the car on the same afternoon, but for different purposes.

You don't need a massive rota to solve such problems, but I can confidently say that a fairly large wall calendar on which each person's essential activities are entered is an enormous help in maintaining domestic peace. Who is going where, and when, and will they be expecting to take the car?

Together, or separately?

Most experts reckon that ideally a couple shouldn't spend *all* their time together. Making space for the other person is important – giving them a degree of independence while you can. Each will have friends who are clearly their own, as well as other 'shared' friends. Each will need to be mature enough to accept that not every relationship is common property.

Of course, the time may come when one partner is entirely dependent on the other, but that profound experience of dependent love and care is best built on the foundation of an already strong relationship of two distinct persons, each with their own dignity and individuality.

In marriage, for instance, the Bible says that the two partners become 'one flesh', but it neither says nor implies that they should lose their own identity as children of God. The miracle of a happy marriage is the voluntary surrender of a bit of our independence in the interests of a greater goal. Retirement may well prove a time to draw closer to our mate, to 'revamp' our marriage, and even to find some of the togetherness and romance we had at first, before work and family commitments came along. It can be an adventure as we get to know our partner all over again. Sadly, retirement can also be a time when 'holes' may show in a marriage, especially when partners have grown apart. If that is the case, counselling, marriage courses or helpful books could be explored (one such is *The Highway Code for Marriage* by Michael and Hilary Perrott, CWR).

The routine of the home

So, on retirement, the routine of the home will inevitably change, but in many ways it will change for the better. For a couple, there will be many shared things – meals, walks, visits to the shops and family outings. There will also be the things each partner does on their own, but not as isolated individuals. Part of true partnership is the daily sharing of events, of people met and things we have seen. It's generally much more fun, for instance, watching TV with someone else rather than on your own.

For the single or widowed person, the home routine will also change. Not only is there suddenly more time, but there are also new possibilities. The skills and experience we acquired during our years of work haven't suddenly evaporated. Now they can, perhaps, be employed in other ways – voluntary work, community or church responsibilities, neighbourhood support schemes and so on. This is not one-sided, either. From such activities we shall make new friends, acquire new interests and enter more fully and satisfyingly into the life of our community.

Ten Commandments for the House Invader **10**

(For simplicity, let's assume the one retiring is male, and the one at home is female.)

1. Go gently. *Pray* your way in. Don't simply walk in and take over the kitchen, the best armchair, the TV remote control, or even the light switches.

2. We are now talking daytime – and weekday daytime at that. Tread warily as you move into unfamiliar territory. Try to feel like a guest at first.

3. Ask if it's OK – is it OK if I walk the dog after lunch? Is it OK if I watch the Test match? Don't make rude remarks about women who watch daytime television. It isn't about 'rights', but about sensitivity. (Equally, women, don't make rude comments about men who just read the paper and watch sport!)

4. Decide what you and your partner will do together, and what things you will do separately. Understand that she may have friends and weekday outings that are long-standing and greatly valued. Respect them.

5. Get out from under her feet! She really won't mind if you spend an afternoon playing golf or indoor bowls.

6. Have a few weekday outings which are regular and planned – a meal out together, or a trip into town or to the shopping mall.

7. Ask if there are any of her activities which you could happily join in with – the local gardening club, for instance, or the gym.

8. Negotiate car use. If necessary, buy a wall calendar and record 'essential' bookings for each user.

9. Offer to do those DIY jobs you've put off for years – the dripping bathroom tap, the squeaky door, the loose bit of carpet on the landing.

10. Plan a nice outing, and over a candlelit meal discuss how your home is going to be a place of perfect partnership. Pray about God's will for you both. You may find God opens doors for you to pray together more, serve together, or to offer hospitality.

Making new friends

If most of our friends were people we had met through work, we may need to find some new ones. Of course we shall continue to keep in touch with close friends made through our employment, but inevitably the absence of that daily contact and shared activity will mean that we see much less of the others. If our workplace was some distance away (as it often is nowadays) then sheer practicality suggests that we shall lose contact with most of our work friends.

In that case – and probably it will be a good thing in the long run – we shall need to find and make friends in our home environment. Church, clubs, neighbours will begin to provide the human setting of our daily lives, and from those situations we shall surely find new friends, or deepen some relationships from acquaintances to true friendship.

It's interesting that we talk about 'making' friends, and it's a fact that generally friendships don't just 'happen'. Friendship has to be sought, welcomed and built. Friendship demands something of us, as well as giving us something that is priceless in itself.

Friendship has to be sought, welcomed and built.

MEMO

Children

Even allowing for the fact that people tend to start their families later nowadays, the probability is that by retirement the children are adult and self-supporting. True, I have friends whose children had not completed college when retirement came for their parents. They were still bringing washing home and expecting the odd financial sub from the new retirees! However, that's unusual. More often the need at retirement is to strike the right note with our adult children. And that's sometimes a tricky one! Do we try to live near them, and risk getting under their feet? Or far away, and risk never seeing them, or any grandchildren? Do we assure them that we're all right health-wise, or let them know that the various niggling problems of advancing years are ours, too – an impending cataract or two, a nasty twinge in the hip, a bit breathless uphill? Do we tell them if we're just the slightest bit anxious about the whole business of retirement, or simply keep quiet?

Naturally, they will be anxious, too. At the time of retirement we're probably all right, but they know that down the line there may eventually be problems. Should they wrap us in cotton wool, fuss about our health or housing or holidays – or just let us get on with it? Do they share their anxieties, or (again) simply keep quiet?

Talking it through

There's quite a lot to say for a really good family discussion about questions of this sort, frank but positive. We don't want to be a 'problem' to them, but we also don't want to pretend that our children and grandchildren aren't an important part of our lives, now and in the future. It would be wrong to hide our anxieties from them entirely, or disregard their anxieties about us.

We shall discuss housing in a later chapter, but working out how we relate to the rest of the family in our new circumstances is a very important issue and well worth thinking through *before* we make a lot of other decisions. Our home may well become a warm and welcome refuge for grandchildren. But not all family set-ups are straightforward.

A word about 'step'

Sadly, many people live in what is euphemistically called 'blended' families, and when we retire we might find our lives far from peaceful as we may be forced to deal with the fallout when children (or grandchildren) have broken relationships. If we are married for the second (or third) time, we may be dealing with stepchildren of our own. This can bring about its own problems in regard to time management, and tension for the retiree. Make sure tha your spiritual life is strong, that you pray with your partner, and that you are lovingly 'together' when there are issues of this sort in your family.

... happiness is much more about relationships than circumstances.

MEMO

The single person

Of course, not all retirees are married and have children or grandchildren. The single person at retirement faces similar but different questions. Friendships are even more important to single people, and those made at work are often lifelong and life-giving. We shall probably want to keep them, which may involve a degree of dedication of time and energy – but it will be worth it. Friendships are there to be treasured, rather than taken for granted.

In retirement, however, we shall find more opportunities to develop other significant friendships. People we have known as nodding acquaintances – at church, perhaps, or as neighbours – may well prove to share interests, values and lifestyle, and from such contacts real and lasting friendships can grow.

We say 'the Greeks have a word for it' – well, they have at least three for love, and one of them, *philadelphia*, is friendship: deep, lasting, committed friendship. That is the kind of love which will be the greatest human gift we can know during the last stage of our lives.

Having said that, many 'young' retirees on their own, perhaps having lost elderly parents they have cared for, decide that they're not too old to find a 'special' friend. There are various options in regard to finding Christian friends of the same or opposite sex, and Christian singles' holidays.

People matter more than things

At retirement – as indeed all through life – it's worth reminding ourselves that, in the end, people matter more than things. One can say categorically that happiness is much more about relationships than circumstances. Who you're with, and who cares about you, is far more important even than *where* you are or how much money you have. Friends and family are the real building blocks of life. At each stage of our journey we need to think hard about how the decisions we make will affect them. (It also needs to be said that some who have given their all to their work or vocation may find that they need to build *new* and substantial friendships at this point in their lives. Not easy, but not impossible.)

Should we move home?

1,2m

arguments for and against moving;
Ten Commandments for Making a Move

Stay, stay at home, my heart, and rest;
Home-keeping hearts are happiest.
(Longfellow)

One of the most pressing immediate problems for many of those facing retirement is the question of relocating.

We may have been in a city or town most of our life, convenient for work, and have cherished for years a vague longing to *Escape to the Country*, as one television programme calls it. Now the possibility is there. Our town or city house is probably worth more than the rural hideaway we have dreamt of. The mortgage may well be paid off. We have no need to stay there for work reasons. So why not sell up and go? It's what thousands of people have done, not just to other parts of Britain, but to France, Spain and even further afield.

Arguments for moving

The most persuasive argument, of course, is that it's possible now, but may never be again. If we don't make such a move while we're still fit and well and full of vigour to strike out and do something new, then we probably never shall. As the kids say, LIVE THE DREAM!

Not only that, but we are at that 'junction' I've talked about, and junctions are where you change trains. Retirement *is* a changing point, and probably a move to a new house will seem a lot less traumatic in the context of this bigger lifestyle change than it would in isolation. We know that we'll probably have to make some new friends anyway, and find some new leisure activities. Moving to a new place, and especially one in a rural or seaside setting, may provide many exciting opportunities for fresh interests. And new neighbours, a new church, or new clubs and associations would surely provide a rich source of new friendships.

If you have lived in one place for many years, you may well feel the need for a change. Again, this would appear to offer the ideal opportunity. Clearly that's what numerous people have felt, and acting on it have sold up and moved on.

For many it has been a good experience. I have several friends who on retirement fulfilled a lifelong dream and moved to France. They seem to have thrived on it, though I have noticed that sometimes one partner is more enthusiastic than the other. Knowing or learning the language helps, of course, and so does a willingness to accept a different culture and lifestyle.

Equally, I have friends who have retired to other parts of Britain – often Devon, Cornwall, Wales or the Scottish Highlands. For most of them it was a really good experience, partly because it was something they'd planned for over a long period, rather than done on a sudden impulse. In those circumstances, there's no doubt that a move to somewhere completely new can be life-enhancing.

The usual advice is not to make any decisions on impulse.

MEMO

Arguments against moving

However, the very differences which make the move attractive to some are the things that make it unappealing to others.

The usual advice is not to make any decisions on impulse. I remember a colleague who, with his wife, had always enjoyed their holidays in a small Cornish seaside town. Suddenly, on retirement, he persuaded her that this was the place where they should live for the rest of their lives.

Sadly, they discovered that the summer suntrap was a winter wetland. Those lovely whitewashed cottages looked very different when the rain set in or the gales blew. Not only that, but it was miles from anywhere – not a problem when all you wanted to do was sit on the beach, but a bit of a handicap when it came to major shopping, hospital clinics and visiting family and friends. They decided in haste, and then found that it was difficult to extricate themselves from what was clearly a bad decision.

But if you are seriously thinking about it, and want to weigh up the pros and cons, what are the contrary indicators to bear in mind?

FAMILY is obviously a big one. Strangely enough, a move to France or Spain may prove less isolating in this respect than a move to another part of the UK. After all, a fortnight's 'holiday' with the grandparents on the Costa del Sol is quite an attractive prospect – and a whole, unbroken fortnight with the children and grandchildren would make up for any number of brief half-day visits.

But the lack of regular contact can be very disappointing. Phone calls, emails and Skype are all very well, but you can't hug an email. Not *too* near, but not *too* far seems to be the best advice for most people.

AMENITIES are another issue. At sixty-five, driving is not too much of a problem for most people. The car may blind us to the fact that there aren't any local buses or trains. I had relatives who left London for rural Suffolk on the man's retirement. They went from a busy London suburb to a beautiful but isolated spot with no public transport. It didn't seem to matter, because they had a car and the wife enjoyed driving. All was well for a few years, until she got bad arthritis and couldn't drive. He had never learnt to do so – not much call for cars in London! Suddenly they were completely cut off. The nearest town was ten miles away; not far, it's true – until the only option would be to walk it or accept a lift.

Important amenities need to be accessible, and in retirement those certainly include the GP's surgery and local hospital, shops, leisure facilities and churches. You can be fairly certain of finding a church almost on your doorstep, but most of the other facilities are only found in towns. *Escape to the Country* can become, in those circumstances, 'Imprisonment in the Home'.

FRIENDS are crucial to our happiness. Often they take years to make but only a week or two to lose, if we move far away. Of course, new friends can be made, but that also takes time. Those who belong to a church or another organisation are more likely to make new friends quickly than those who are not 'joiners'.

Of course we will intend to keep our old friends, and probably we shall keep contact with them faithfully. But what we need most from friends is company, chats, laughs – and shared tears, sometimes. That's not so easy when we don't actually see them.

CHURCH is very important to people of faith. Often the church we belong to is the single most important ingredient of our social well-being, a kind of spiritual haven for the storms of life. Before deciding on a move, it would be wise to examine the church situation where you are planning to go. The transition can be painless, indeed even rewarding – but equally it can be a rather slow process of settling in, making new friends and becoming accustomed, perhaps, to a different way of doing things. (There may not be a church of our preferred denomination in our new location). Not to have thought through and prayed seriously about how a move would affect our church affiliation is hardly 'taking faith seriously'.

LONG-TERM prospects are also worth thinking about. If you are married, and one of you becomes ill and dependent, what kind of support will you get? While the new location might be very satisfying while you are a couple, if one of you is left alone, what will happen?

We have really been dealing here with couples. For singles, moving to a strange place where they know no one and starting again could be very daunting. A single person might consider a move to be near extended family. However, we would have to think about what and who we are leaving behind. Lifelong friends can sometimes become like family for those who are on their own.

The choice is yours!

It's important to stress that just as there are no infallible arguments *for* moving, there are no irrefutable arguments *against* it. The decision is yours, after careful thought. And, in fact, most people who move find that in the end it was the right thing to do, just as most people who stay put are glad they did!

Ten Commandments for Making a Move

1. Set down the reasons for doing it.

2. Show them to the other person/s involved. Do they agree? (If you are on your own, show a friend.)

3. Set down any reasons *not* to move.

4. Show them to the others involved. Do they share them? (And if you are single, again talk this through with a friend, spiritual mentor or pastor.)

5. Don't make a hasty decision. Wait at least six months.

6. Take your time about choosing the new house.

7. Check whether the new house is near shops or on a bus route (the time may come when you can't drive a car).

8. Consider how convenient it will be for visiting/ being visited by family and friends.

9. What about church?

10. If it's right, go for it. It won't be easier in five years' time. Be sure to let everyone know!

Being retired

$^{1}2m$

avoiding the negative track; staying fully
alive; exercising the brain cells; exploring
'outside the box'; three ages of retirement

Being retired

I am Retired Leisure. I am to be met with in trim gardens. I am already come to be known by my vacant face and careless gesture, perambulating at no fixed pace nor with any settled purpose. I walk about, not to or from.
(Charles Lamb, *The Superannuated Man*)

There's no doubt some people – mostly younger ones – do tend to think of retirees in the terms described there by Charles Lamb. They see them about the town, sitting on park benches or walking their dogs in an aimless kind of way, and assume that's what being retired is like. It is, they observe, a life without object or purpose, vacant and pointless. Once you reach that stage, they think, you might as well bypass the intervening years and go straight to the Great Beyond. 'Do not pass GO, do not collect £200.'

MEMO
It's not about what you *do* when you're retired ...

You'll notice that this chapter is called 'being' retired. It's not about what you *do* when you're retired, or how you plan for retirement, whether you move home, or how your nearest and dearest feel about it. It's about you, or me, retired: what we *are*.

The same person

It's quite important to be clear that you're the same person as you were the day before you stopped

working. We might say, the goods are the same; all that
has changed is the packaging. Retirement is a lifestyle
change, and that's all it is.

Avoiding the negative track

Sadly, for a few people it manages to become much
more than that. They feel cut off, isolated, diminished.
No longer what they *were*, they become unsure what
they *are* – especially if they defined themselves by their
job or career. They can become moody or withdrawn,
and touchy about discussing it, even with their partner.
If this state of mind persists, it can lead to depression.

To avoid going down that very negative track, it
helps to talk through your feelings with either a good
and wise friend (but *not* someone very close to you),
or even a professional counsellor.

In mourning for the past

As you talk, you may begin to see that your gloomy
feelings are little more than the consequence of the
difficulty of adapting to a new lifestyle. You have lost
something – a job you enjoyed, or a set of colleagues
who provided daily stimulus and fun – and so far you
haven't found anything to replace it. In effect, you have
been *bereaved*. You are in mourning for the past, instead
of enjoying the present and making plans for the future.

However, while some undoubtedly get into that state
of mind, not all do. But it's quite common, on retirement,
to feel what we may describe as 'withdrawal symptoms',
especially if our work has been largely satisfying and
rewarding.

COUNTERING THE 'WITHDRAWAL':
Some ideas:
Ask, what has really changed?
Look to the future, not the past.

Think of the advantages of the present.
Turn regrets into gratitude. (They were good years at
work, cherish the memories.)
Shower the people you love with love!

> *It is very grand to die in harness, but it is very*
> *pleasant to have the tight straps unbuckled and*
> *the heavy collar lifted from the neck and shoulders*
> Oliver Wendell Holmes, *Over The Teacups*

Staying fully alive

After a lifetime of work, possibly in a job where the brain
as well as the body was kept active and alert, retirement
can be the signal for a kind of mental and physical switch-
off. After a suitable break, we settle back into home life,
but often that does not – in fact, cannot – provide us with
the kind of mental stimulus a daily job does. Whether you
were a barrister or a baker, work meant keeping alert,
on top of things. The alternative would be crooks getting
away with it, and cottage loaves without roofs.

It's quite natural to see retirement as a respite from
the daily demands of work, but we shall live to regret
it if the result is that our brainpower diminishes and
we lose our appetite for life. True, there is no employer
demanding that we complete a task; no customer
requiring us to reach certain standards; no great
necessity to meet deadlines or complete a task on
time. If the garden needs weeding, it could be done
today, or tomorrow, or next week, if the mood requires
it. Why not just let it wait? There's always tomorrow …

It's worth mentioning here, too, the importance of
keeping as fit and healthy as possible for the sake of
our physical *and* mental well-being.

Keep alert!

These are the danger signals of Retirement Decline!
Unchecked, they can lead to a life without shape or

meaning, and a brain rusty with disuse. We don't need to invent a kind of substitute work regime, but most people benefit from a recognisable pattern of daily life.

Not a timetable

It's true that some retired people take this to extremes. I have often listened to recitals of a daily routine which sounds as regimented as the worst workplace. 'Oh, we always wake with the seven o'clock news. Then Tom goes down and makes tea. We drink that in bed, and then we get up. Alternate days, each has the exclusive use of the bathroom and the one not using it gets the breakfast. We put on *The Morning Show* while we have breakfast. Then I make the bed while he washes up …' And so it goes on, right through the day, so that they can tell you exactly what they'll be doing each day of the week – the hairdresser on Tuesdays, the midweek service on Wednesdays, Tesco's (on the free bus) on Fridays, and so on.

You don't need a kind of prison camp timetable to have a shape to life, however. And you don't need to watch TV all day to keep the brain cells working (quite the opposite, sometimes).

Creating a shape

Each retired person will have their own idea of an ideal 'shape' to daily life. Sometimes that shape will emerge naturally from our own choices and lifestyle. Sometimes we shall need to think about it, and decide in our own minds what our new daily pattern will be. That's not, I hope, going to involve a strict daily timetable as inflexible as that of the life of daily work, but an emerging custom to give an outline to our daily life within which we can enjoy a lot of variety.

In my case, I have found that the shape of a typical day has emerged from the kind of things I do and the needs of daily life. After breakfast, the one absolutely fixed point of the day is prayer and Bible reading. Personally, I use what's called the 'Daily Office', a pattern of readings, set prayers and spontaneous reflection and worship – it takes about twenty minutes. After that I spend most mornings at my computer, writing. It's my hobby, just as gardening or painting are for others. After lunch I tend to do the household chores – washing, cleaning, tending the small garden, that kind of thing. Then later on if there's any shopping to do I slip out to do it. Evenings are either for television or social and church events.

That pattern is not inflexible, by any means – apart from the prayer time – but at least it gives me a reason to get up in the morning. There is a real danger, as one gets older, in not having one!

Weekends are important, as they were during working life, but for different reasons. Now they are not so much a break from the routine of work, as an opportunity to spend time with the younger members of our family, children and grandchildren especially. Needless to say they are also the prime times for other activities – sport, clubs and societies and church, for example.

MEMO

As with our physical fitness, mental fitness does depend on exercise.

Exercising the brain cells

I had a friend, now dead, who, well into his eighties, would do *The Times* crossword every morning. He kept a record of how long it took, reckoning that impending mental decline would then immediately become apparent. To the day he died, approaching ninety, the figure remained much the same, though the occasional day would lead him to incoherent fury at the expense of the unknown crossword setter.

As with our physical fitness, mental fitness does

depend on exercise. We don't wear the brain out with use, but stimulate its effectiveness.

Many retired people have rediscovered the local library. What a fantastic source of mental stimulation and pleasure is to be found there – and it's usually free. A couple of hours with a book every day will not only provide a rich feast of story, image and ideas, but a book is entirely portable, unlike the TV.

For those of us who see our whole life as a gift of God, it is important to remember that word 'whole'. Right to its end, life is God's gift – we are just stewards of it. It would be entirely wrong to regard any part of the life we have been given as superfluous, unimportant or pointless.

Exploring 'outside the box'

Retirement gives us the opportunity to expand our thinking – as the saying goes, to move 'outside the box'. The 'box' is our usual realm, the familiar world of ideas we have always known. But now there is time to explore! You don't have to be an intellectual to do this: in fact, that might even be a disadvantage. Thinking outside the box simply means exploring things we've never had time for previously, or perhaps felt were 'not quite us'.

Spiritual enquiry

For many people, thinking 'outside the box' takes them into the area of spiritual enquiry. Perhaps you've never been conventionally 'religious', but now there's the opportunity to explore the whole world of faith. I've known many people who in retirement began by slipping into empty churches and just enjoying the silence and peace. They then started occasionally going to services, or listening to sacred music. Beyond that, they visited a monastery or two, even perhaps staying for a couple of days' quiet and contemplation. After that – well, anything is possible!

You may feel that doesn't sound like your kind of thing – but you'll never know if you don't try it.

The three ages of retirement

It's quite easy to recognise three common stages in the process of retirement. Each stage has its pleasures and its drawbacks, and of course not everybody goes through all of them. Once upon a time – not all that long ago – many people died early in retirement. Pension schemes were based on the principle that a high proportion of retirees would only draw their pension for a short period. My own father died before he could start drawing his pension.

Now, however, an averagely healthy man or woman reaching sixty-five can reasonably expect around fifteen years or more of life. It's that extended period of retirement that's putting a strain on pension funds, of course, and it's also the reason why we can now see three stages of retirement for many people.

MEMO

... for those who are fit and healthy, it can be a time of 'doing'.

Stage 1: Activity

The first years of retirement for many people are a time of almost endless activity, depending of course on the age and health of the retiree. But for those who are fit and healthy, it can be a time of 'doing'. Visits that had long been planned, holidays in the UK and abroad, more time in the garden, new hobbies, active membership of clubs and societies, public responsibilities happily accepted – you wonder where they find the time to do it all. The truth is, there is pent-up energy available. Just because daily work has ceased it doesn't mean that mental and physical 'engines' have been switched off. It's quite natural that the person whose days were previously occupied with the demands of a daily job should find, on retirement, the need for some outlet for skills, enthusiasm and interests.

These are the 'newly retired', without whom clubs, churches, societies and charities would probably cease to function.

Stage 2: Enjoying leisure

Again, depending on the age at which they have retired, and health issues, after five or ten years of such activity, most retired people begin to slow down. That's not to say they're 'past it', but somewhere after the age of seventy the mind and the body begin to need some tender loving care. So the retired person enters the period I've called 'enjoying leisure'. They gracefully resign from any leadership roles: churchwarden or deacon, chair of local clubs, organiser of a sports' league, secretary of the parish council, school governor.

That doesn't mean they don't do anything, but that they feel the time has come to let others take the responsibility while they learn how to put their feet up occasionally. Walking the dog, meeting friends for coffee, going to church, being a club member rather than leader: this is the way the members of stage 2 may see their lives.

In some ways this is how many younger people see retirement from day one, but actually it's very much the *second* stage in most cases. This is when retired people turn to family and friends, not reluctantly but gladly. The peace of hearth and home may seem preferable to endless committees, battles over this and that, account books, club minutes and organising coffee mornings. The time may well come when they seem preferable even to the hassle of organising a personal holiday!

Stage 3: The last lap

*'Even to your old age and grey hairs I am he, I am
he who will sustain you. I have made you and I will
carry you; I will sustain you and I will rescue you.'*
(Isaiah 46:4)

Assuming we make it that far, all of us will inevitably
move on to the third stage of retirement, the 'Last Lap'.
The next chapter looks more closely at the issue of
aging, but what is certain is that time ticks remorselessly
towards the final lap. It's foolish to put a date on this,
because people vary so much. Indeed, a few people live
to a great old age and *never* seem to reach it!

> **MEMO**
>
> **Old age has its
> compensations.**

   Nevertheless, most of us face the fact that
eventually, if we survive, we shall be genuinely
'elderly'. On the whole, it's not something we look
forward to. If we are financially secure and relatively
healthy, we can see the appeal of the years of active
retirement, full of energy, and of the leisurely stage that
we hope will follow it. But we are anxious about the
coming of the time when we can no longer get about,
look after ourselves in a satisfactory kind of way, and
even perhaps remember which day of the week it is.

   There are two things to say about this. Old age
has its compensations. On the whole, people are
nice to you. No one expects you to rush around, take
responsibility or meet deadlines. Provided one is
largely pain-free, and the mind is sound (even if the
brain cells take a bit longer to register sometimes), one
can learn to enjoy different pleasures: family, friends,
conversation, the radio. Prayer and reflection are other
great gifts to those who can no longer be fully active.

This can also be a time for passing on our wisdom to the young, and simply listening.

The other compensation is philosophical. We have nothing left to prove. All that we were to do, we have done, for better or worse. There is no need to rebuke ourselves for missed opportunities. They are part of the past, not the present, and certainly not the future. Our sole challenge now is to turn any regrets into grateful memories. And memories, let there be no doubt about it, are the chief delight of the elderly. We've got plenty of them.

Growing older gracefully

$\frac{1}{2}$m

as old as you feel; moving on with the years; pointless regrets; facing the final junction; Ten Commandments for Growing Older Gracefully

Growing older gracefully

Old age has its pleasures which, though different, are not less than the pleasures of youth.
(W. Somerset Maugham, *The Summing-Up*)

They will still bear fruit in old age, they will stay fresh and green, proclaiming, 'The LORD is upright; he is my Rock, and there is no wickedness in him.'
(Psalm 92:14–15)

One possible consequence of stopping work is the realisation that we have got older. It's funny how for years and years we can largely disregard this strange fact. We don't *feel* older (inside our heads, we're all still in our twenties!), but when we're 'retired' we may find ourselves contemplating the fact that we *are*.

It doesn't help when, certainly in the UK, newspapers and other people talk about 'Old Age Pensioners' (OAPs). The phrase went out of official use decades ago, but it's strange how it has stuck in popular usage. 'OAP in accident at zebra crossing' screams the headline. Read the story, and you find that a sixty-five-year-old woman was on her way to a tennis match when she encountered a bus in the high street.

To have a pension is not necessarily to be 'old' – and ages of retirement differ – though obviously when we reach that stage we are 'older' than we were before. How we deal with the fact of advancing years then becomes a crucial factor in our happiness, or the lack of it.

Being my age

When we were teenagers our parents probably sometimes told us, 'Be your age!' – meaning we should act like a sensible fifteen-year-old, and not a toddler. The same advice, however, applies all through life. It doesn't mean that because I am seventy I should behave like a stereotype of a seventy-year-old, but that there is a style appropriate to each phase of life, and we look ridiculous if we blatantly flout that convention. Having said that, there are definitely some older people who 'act outside the box'. One man, in his sixties, after being involved in renovating a house in France, bought a sporty left-hand drive Chevrolet Camaro. Another, in his eighties, was sent to the seaside for a 'rest' and finished up actively involved in evangelism on the seafront.

... we shall have to face the stark facts of our birth certificate.

MEMO

As old as you feel?

'You're as old as you feel', we say, which is usually true. If we are basically fit and active, we shall not feel 'old'. Indeed, nobody in the society I live in thinks of sixty-five or even seventy as 'old'. Inevitably, however, if we find some of the conditions of aging appearing in our lives, we shall have to face the stark facts of our birth certificate.

I would have to admit that when people say to me 'You're as old as you feel' my reaction is dictated by present circumstances. Sometimes, on a good day, when everything's gone well, I suppose I feel – well, sixty-something. But on a bad day, when the wind's cold and I've stubbed my toe in the bathroom or nicked my chin while shaving I feel more like ninety.

However old we 'feel', at some point we shall need to slow down a bit. It's pointless to think that we can do at seventy or eighty what we did at sixty. In any case, it isn't wise to try.

Moving on with the years

There is nothing wrong – it's not a sin, even a little one – with having a bit of a snooze after lunch, for instance. As we get older we may find that we wake earlier in the morning than we used to (though I never have). Equally, we may find that long drawn-out social events tend to be a bit exhausting. Again, it's not a sin to make a polite excuse and leave at a sensible time. There's no point in fighting advancing years.

Holding back the march of time

On the other hand, we don't have to collude with them. A healthy diet, a sensible amount of exercise, plenty of interests and pursuits, and a few things to look forward to will go a long way to holding back the relentless march of time.

A friend of mine in his mid-eighties had always wanted to surf, and finally got the opportunity. Donning a wetsuit, taking a short lesson, and screwing up his courage, he carried his surfboard out into the waters off a Devon beach – and successfully surfed his way in, several times. Not everyone of his age could do it, but most of us could probably do more than we expect if we try.

Pointless regrets

'Being my age' simply means acting genuinely as I feel, not trying to put on a performance in a desperate attempt to kid myself and others that I'm still in my fifties. But it also means living fully and positively, making the most of the time God has given me, rather than wasting time on pointless regrets or complaining that 'I can't do what I used to do'.

Facing the final junction

If – as I've constantly done – we think of life as a journey, and retirement as a junction where we 'change trains', then we are all, of course, aware that there's one more 'junction' ahead. Many younger people can, and do, ignore the subject of death completely, but as we know we're approaching the end of the journey of life, it's natural sometimes to think about it – even to dread the very thought of it.

Strangely, in my experience, few old people actually worry about death. It's dying – the process, not the event – that troubles them. In fact, with modern healthcare very few people die in serious pain. As a minister, I've often sat by the bedside of a dying person and I can say that it is usually a peaceful and even inspiring experience. Most of us naturally reach a point – if we live that long – where we feel that it's 'time to go', and when that time comes we accept that death is, in fact, part of life.

Of course, a strong Christian faith is a transforming element in facing the final 'junction'. The Bible, and especially Jesus Himself, is quite clear that the process of death is not the end of the human journey. Jesus told us that 'Those who believe in me will live, even though they die; and everyone who lives and believes in me will never die' (John 11:25–26, NRSV), and so the apostle Paul could speak of death as a gateway to something that was 'better by far' (Philippians 1:23).

This is, of course, a matter of faith, and some find it easier to believe than others. But to have faced, in whatever way we choose, the reality of death is an important step to a peaceful old age. For me, the hope of life beyond death, in the company of a loving God and (in some way) of those I have loved on earth, is enormously sustaining and reassuring.

If this is an issue you would like to pursue, why not make a point of talking about it to a Christian minister, or a sympathetic believing friend?

An undeserved gift

To 'grow old gracefully', as people used to put it, doesn't mean simply 'growing old', but moving on through the years in a 'graceful' way.

'Grace' is a wonderful word. It actually means an undeserved gift – its original use was to describe God's attitude to us. Life itself, and all its good things, such as love, joy, hope and faith, are His gift. To see the whole of our life as a gift helps us to appreciate it, not taking it for granted but gratefully treasuring the passing years as a bonus for the evening of life. Once we see them in this way, we shall stop moaning about being old and accept thankfully the time we've been given – time for friends and family, for hobbies and interests, for new interests and pursuits; time for good things we never seemed to have time for during our working lives. That's 'growing older gracefully'.

Ten Commandments for Growing Older Gracefully

1. Face facts – your birth certificate doesn't lie!
2. Be your age, not someone else's.
3. Slow down a bit (but not too much).
4. Take regular exercise – minimum thirty minutes a day.
5. Try to do a word-based puzzle (such as a crossword) every day.
6. Cultivate friends of all ages, including young ones.
7. Live positively.
8. Consider the spiritual aspects of growing older; explore issues of faith, if you never have.
9. Come to terms with the present – and the future.
10. Be grateful: count your blessings – your life is a precious gift.

Some case studies

$\frac{1}{2}$m

Tony, Mary, Harry, Anita, Robert and Phyllis's stories

… too much rest itself becomes a pain.
(Homer, from *The Odyssey*)

Based on real-life stories, these examples at least show the variety of ways in which people can experience retirement.

Tony's story

TONY wouldn't even talk about retirement. For him, it represented the end of everything he valued. All he could see beyond the end of his working life was boredom and frustration. He was a craftsman, he said, and his main pride and joy in life was what he could make. What he actually made was bread – prize-winning, top class, wholesome, nutritious, beautiful bread. He'd won many prizes, and people came from miles around to buy their bread at his bakery in a small Berkshire village.

When friends, or his anxious wife, asked him when he was thinking of stopping work, he would reply, 'Never. I shall die with flour on my hands.' His home, his family, his friends all took second, third and fourth places to his beloved bread, or rather his 'craft', as he called it. Without that, he felt he would be a nobody.

In fact, he very nearly *did* die with flour on his hands. They found him collapsed by his oven. He recovered from the heart attack, but was still reluctant to accept the inevitable. Surely now, those closest to him pleaded, he would see sense and retire. It wasn't until the doctor told him that if he went on working nine or ten hours a day he would inevitably have another, and probably fatal, attack that he reluctantly agreed, though it took a grand combined effort by family and friends to keep him away from the bakery.

He didn't like it, of course. But he did occasionally admit that perhaps it was getting a bit beyond him (he was over seventy when he stopped work). More importantly, after his best friend, George, introduced him to the delights of the riverside, Tony found that the skill and patience that made him a good baker also made him a good fisherman.

It was also (he grudgingly admitted) quite nice to have time for the family – two generations of them, with a third on the way – and to rediscover what good company his wife of forty-five years could be.

He never admitted to actually *liking* retirement, but at least he learnt that there is life after the end of work – even work as deeply satisfying as making top-quality bread.

Mary's story

MARY had trained as a nurse, and had spent most of her working life in community nursing – district nurse, and then health visitor. It had been an absorbing career, much more than just her 'daily work'. Her clients had become her friends, and she knew many of the people in her neighbourhood because she had shared important moments of life with them. She had never married, but she had many lifelong friends, dating back to her training hospital days.

When her time for retirement came, she was rather anxious. Her work was her life – or, at any rate, a big part of it. She simply couldn't imagine living without the constant contact with people, and the wonderful feeling of being appreciated and valued. She wondered what on earth she would do with her time when there was no longer a caseload to consider, visits to make, clinic appointments to keep.

Her other main interests were centred around her church. She'd been a very committed Christian from her teens, and was a familiar figure in the Baptist church in her town. Because of her work commitments she had never been able to take on other responsibilities in the church, but everyone accepted that she was already fully engaged in what they recognised as a vital vocation. If anybody fulfilled the command about 'loving your neighbour', it was surely Mary.

MEMO 'This is exactly what I had always hoped it might be like!'

In fact, when she retired she first took a holiday with her old friend Jane, visiting (for the first time in her life) the Scottish Highlands. Then she took a month or two coming to terms with her new lifestyle, but soon felt that she had too much energy and enthusiasm to waste it sitting around the house. So she let it be known that, after forty years, she was ready to take on a 'job' at the church.

Needless to say, her offer was eagerly taken up. The church arranged for her to undertake a short training course, and she then joined the pastoral team as a support worker, visiting people in their homes, helping them in times of crisis or anxiety, and running a small support group for single mums. Her verdict on retirement now is that 'This is exactly what I had always hoped it might be like!'

Harry's story

HARRY retired at the end of a rather mixed working life. Leaving school in the 1960s without any particular qualifications, he got a job as a postman. He liked the open air part of it, and that once he'd collected the mail it was up to him to organise how he did his deliveries. When, five years later, he married, he changed his job, driving a delivery van. Again he liked the freedom, but could see that it was not exactly a career. Neither was his next job, working as a groundsman at the local sports park, or the one after that, as caretaker at the local junior school.

Yet he enjoyed his work. He was, he supposed, a bit of a 'loner'; he preferred to plan his own day's work and wasn't very worried that his jobs didn't involve much contact with colleagues. He enjoyed going home at the end of the day, but he realised that all through his working life he hadn't really spent a great deal of time with his wife, Carol, or with his two sons.

When retirement drew near, several things worried him. None of his jobs had gone far towards providing a satisfactory pension. Carol had worked as a teaching assistant at a local school and was not yet due for retirement, but he thought money might be a problem.

More than that, though, he worried about his relationships. How would it be when he was at home every day? How would he get on with Carol in their new circumstances? And as for his sons, both of whom had partners and families, would he be able to rebuild a good relationship with them?

The best thing was that at least he saw the problems. He talked it over with Carol; probably the first time they'd had a conversation of that kind. They arranged to visit his sons – they both lived in other parts of the country – and that proved very rewarding.

It would be wrong to say that he had a painless transition to retirement. However, both his major worries proved unfounded. They had enough money – though not so much, as Carol pointed out, that they could 'go mad'. And life at home was not a problem once they had sorted out a few ground rules!

Harry joined an indoor bowls club and, later on, Carol went along, too. They made some good friends there – probably the first Harry had made since he left school.

Anita's story

ANITA was a doctor. After graduation she had decided that she would complete her medical training as a GP.

She had enjoyed her work – thirty years of it, with a break in the middle when her two children were little. She had rather dreaded retirement, knowing that she and her husband, Ralph, had very different interests. Sadly, however, he died of a heart attack soon after he retired and just before she was due to end work. That left her on her own. The children were married and living far away.

The first months of retirement were very difficult. Tears for Ralph, and the years they would not spend together; regret that her life's work was over, and the feeling that whereas previously she was clearly of value to many people, now she was simply 'retired'.

It was one Sunday during a church service that an answer came. Her church supported medical clinics in Lesotho, an African kingdom with problems of poverty and disease. A representative of the organisation spoke about their need of qualified doctors and nurses to help with this work, and for Anita it was like a personal invitation. She spoke to the man afterwards, and within a month or two was on her way to Africa, able to use her medical training, but in a very different setting from the suburban surgery she had worked in previously. When she eventually came back to Britain, it was with a completely new view of the world we live in, and of her own place in it.

Robert's story

ROBERT had had a hard life. Adopted as a baby by an older couple, both of whom had died before he was twenty, he felt insecure and vulnerable as a young adult. His schooling had been a bit of a muddle – several different schools, little encouragement to study at home and a number of bouts of illness meant that he had little to show for his years of education.

Possibly as a result, he had never really settled into any job. Mostly they lasted for only a few months, which meant that potential employers were reluctant to give him another chance. Periods of unemployment were broken by spells in various jobs, few of them particularly rewarding.

When retirement time came, Robert had no idea what life would hold for him. He had no family that he knew of, and few real friends. He lived in a tiny flat over a shop and wondered how he would continue to pay the rent.

He took to spending most of his mornings in the public library. He'd always enjoyed reading – mostly about facts, how things worked, history, stories of real people. And it was warm in there, too.

It was in the library that he met Janet, an older woman who also found the library a congenial place to pass the time. She was a cheerful person, very well-read – her late husband had been a history teacher. She found Robert a kindred spirit, even though he had missed out on much of his formal education. It was an unusual but mutually rewarding friendship, which ended up with them often going on excursions together to places of historical interest.

This was a new world for Robert, and a new kind of relationship. With Janet around, retirement actually seemed fun. That was something he had never even contemplated. They joined the University of the Third Age (U3A) and for the first time in his life Robert felt that he was 'somebody'. When he got a diploma for a research project they did together on historical sites in Lincolnshire, he *knew* he was!

Phyllis's story

PHYLLIS had never been employed, but that didn't mean she hadn't worked hard. Husband Tom had worked all their married lives until now, and she had seen it as her responsibility to look after the house, do the shopping, keep the household accounts and (most demanding of all) bring up their three children. All of this she had done faithfully and well.

Now Tom's work was ending, but she knew that in one sense hers never would. True, the children had fled the nest, but the house seemed to get bigger and bigger as she got older, and there always seemed plenty to do. It was lovely to see the family when they came to stay, but there was no denying that it created a lot of work for her – not that she minded.

However, most of all she worried about Tom's retirement. Work had meant so much to him. He didn't have any real hobbies, he didn't read much, and he even got bored with the television (which she never did).

It was a bit difficult at first, when it happened. She tried to remember not to let him see how hard it was for her to have a second person in the house on weekdays, though she appreciated the extra pair of hands in the supermarket. Slowly they worked out a new style of life, sometimes planning little outings – days out, that sort of thing – and visits to the children and grandchildren.

Best of all, as a couple, they found that they were making friendships with other couples, something they'd never done before. Phyllis began to feel she could enjoy this retirement business after all.

What's good about being retired?

^{1}2m

do something new; memories; celebrating love and discovering past affection; doing some mending; discovering the real 'me'; asking the big questions; The Ten Commandments (Final Version)

Life is the greatest bargain. We get it for nothing
(Yiddish Proverb)

*I'd like to know what this whole show is all about
before it's out*
(Piet Hein)

*For the complete life, the perfect pattern includes
old age as well as youth, and maturity*
(W. Somerset Maugham)

*[God] has made everything suitable for its time;
moreover, he has put a sense of past and future
into their minds … I know that there is nothing
better for them than to be happy and enjoy
themselves as long as they live …*
(Ecclesiastes 3:11–12, NRSV)

As you may have gathered, I don't think being retired
is a bad thing. In fact, disregarding a few stumbles on
the way, my own twenty-plus years of it have been
very happy and rewarding. In considering specially
what's *good* about retirement, I've tried to look at the
general scene, rather than simply rehearse my own
experiences, but I'm confident that many of the positive
things I shall describe are familiar elements of the life
of many retired people.

Do something new!

All through life, human beings are intrigued by new
things – new gadgets, new clothes, new games, even
new programmes on the television. It's almost as

though we are programmed to seek out what is new – which may be why it is a theme in the Bible that God is constantly doing 'new things', 'making everything new'.

Retirement offers us the opportunity to do something completely new. There will be time and opportunities, if we seize them. A new hobby, a new interest in life, a new commitment: it's amazing the difference they can make to the way we feel about ourselves. It can be life-changing, dynamic!

I have seen retired men and women take up painting or gardening or hill-walking. I have a friend who after a lifetime as a builder and decorator bought himself his first computer, joined the local history society and became an expert in the story of the area where he lived. Not only that, but he began to research his own family history, producing astonishing results through diligent and painstaking research.

Doing something new is, or may seem to be, a bit of a risk – we might fall flat on our faces. But surely that's the whole point of it. We *know* we can do what we've always done, the challenge is to do something we've *never* done before. In case you can't think of anything new that you'd like to do, here are a few ideas:

THINGS YOU MIGHT TRY:

- Cooking
- Painting or pottery (local art classes)
- U3A (local branches)
- Computing, using the internet, Skype (local classes); learning how to blog online, social media
- Learning a language (tapes and CDs, local groups)
- Joining a walking group
- Taking short trips by coach to interesting places
- Getting an allotment
- Joining a local dramatic group
- Taking on volunteer work in your area
- Joining a choir
- Taking an interest in local politics
- Investigating your family history
- Giving church a try …

- … or trying a different denomination/style of worship!
- Reading to the blind
- Taking dancing lessons
- Taking up a new sport – even a challenging one such as fencing or archery!
- Regularly joining with friends to enjoy trips to the cinema or theatre
- Doing or helping on an Alpha course
- Making models: cars, boats, houses, planes
- Getting a pet … adopting an older, unwanted dog if a puppy would prove too much!
- Joining a photography class
- Getting a senior rail card and visiting all those places you've heard of but never seen
- Learning a musical instrument
- Taking a writing course and planning the novel you have always wanted to write
- Investigating the possibilities of mission …
- … or other areas of Christian service and outreach

MEMO The one thing every retired person has is plenty of memories.

Make the most of your memories

The one thing every retired person has is plenty of memories. They are the most precious resource of the passing years. Some may be painful at first, but often those are the very ones we need to cherish and store up. Memory can lead us down so many wonderful roads.

Without leaving your armchair you can travel back through time, to childhood and schooldays. You can recall old friends and glorious holidays. You can relive the excitement of first love, the amazing miracle of the birth of children, fulfilling spiritual experiences, happy times with loved ones. Without moving, you can be in all the favourite places you have ever visited – that football stadium, that dance floor, that country pub long ago, that blissful beach – and be with those you have loved, in your mind. Sitting there, you can capture afresh the laughter of children, the tears of parting, weddings, baptisms, graduation days, parties, picnics, and special moments. Memories are for keeping, and one of the best things about the time offered by retirement is that you can set to and store them up.

Among them, as I've said, will be some that are painful – the loss of a deeply loved partner, parent, brother, sister or friend for instance. But they are still precious. We wouldn't want to forget them. What we can do with those sorts of memories, however, is to turn regrets into gratitude. The people and events we remember – all of them – are part of the life we have lived, part of our treasury of experiences. To keep saying 'thank you' as the pictures from the past flit like scenes in a film before the eye of memory is to transform them.

Cherish your memories!

Some people create a literal scrapbook of memories, complete with photos, press cuttings, old letters and greeting cards. A few I have known have actually written an autobiography and had it published – mainly for friends and family, it's true, but everyone's story, as local journalists know, is interesting. There are a number of publishers who specialise in producing autobiographies on a small scale.

An autobiography doesn't have to appear in print, of course. Other people I know of have sat in front of a microphone and recorded their memories, creating a kind of sound archive of times past. And there is also the option of 'blogging' your memories on the internet – see for example **www.blogger.com**

Celebrating love

Love is the most precious of all the gifts of life, and one of the advantages of retirement is time and space to celebrate it. Often during our working lives we lose contact with people we are fond of, not by choice but simply because there is not enough time to keep in regular touch with them. Now there is time to look at your Christmas cards in a new way. These are voices from our past – people we have known and, in some cases, been very close to, but now our only contact is the annual ritual of the card at Christmas.

DISCOVER THE WARMTH AND AFFECTION OF THE PAST

Well, there is now the opportunity, surely, to pick out the ones we should really like to do something about – to renew our relationship, to discover if the warmth and affection of the past is still there. By doing this, I met up with a man I hadn't seen for over sixty years, since we used to cycle to school together in Wales. It was amazing to find how much we still had in common, and how strong the bond of friendship still was. Another long-lost friendship restored was a contact from my National Service days in the RAF – we'd been the entire medical staff at a busy airfield in Hampshire, and both sang in the local opera group.

You might find the new social media helpful here – such as Friends Reunited, or even the dreaded Facebook!

EXPRESS IT!

Part of the process of celebrating love is to express it. Tell people you like them. Be open about how much their friendship means to you. Now, in the expansive evening of life, make the most of love and friendship – not only old friends, but family. Dispel any idea that you're an old fogey who can't stand a bit of noise, and enjoy their company!

Doing some mending

In most people's lives there are incidents and events which we deeply regret, and often they lead to broken or strained relationships. Years and years ago something was said or done, by us or by them, which broke a friendship or strained a family relationship. Now, in the retirement years, there may be the opportunity to do some remedial work – to try, at least, to mend such broken relationships and to be reconciled with those from whom we have become estranged.

Of course, it isn't easy. Both parties would need to want reconciliation. Apologies would be needed; it's never very easy to say 'sorry' (especially if deep down we don't feel it was entirely our fault). But the prize is worth the pain. It would be sad to come to our life's end still at odds with a close relative or a once-precious friend. Someone has to make the first move. Let it be me!

Discovering the real 'me'

It's possible to reach retirement hidden behind life's labels – 'Mum', 'Dad', 'Grandma', 'the boss', 'the carer' (especially if we have had elderly parents to look after) and so on – as though we're playing a part in someone else's play. It's probably unavoidable up to this point, because not only is that how others see us, but it's how we have seen ourselves.

Retirement provides a great opportunity to throw aside the labels and discover who we *really* are – the 'me' that lurks behind the roles the Casting Director of life has assigned to us; I may no longer be the boss, or the nurse, or the bus driver, but I am (much more importantly) a child of God, made in His image and valued by Him.

We can actually at this point work at being *ourselves*. This might sound rather selfish or self-centred, but in fact it is often a step towards being a much more rounded, contented and fulfilled person, and consequently better company, more outgoing and altogether nicer to know.

NEEDED: TIME, AND PERSONAL HONESTY

To find the inner 'me' requires some time, and a degree of personal honesty. If you can manage a few quiet days away, it helps. Spend some of that time, at least, reviewing your life so far. What has given you the greatest pleasure? What worries you the most? Are you better in company, or alone? What sorts of things irritate you intensely, and what kinds of things give you most satisfaction?

As you think about the next few years, are there things you dread (try to be honest with yourself), and are there things you look forward to? How good are you at close relationships? With whom do you most enjoy spending time?

It's not a bad idea to write down your conclusions, and try to see whether a picture emerges of the real 'you' – not the one who tries hard to like people, or struggles not to be bored in company, but the person that you know you are deep down ('warts and all', as they say).

MEMO

We like questions – but we prefer answers.

Asking the big questions

Life is full of big questions, but while we're busy with other things we can safely ignore them. Still, they're there, and most of us wonder, from time to time, what the answers might be. Why is there *anything* rather than nothing? What do we mean by eternity? Is there a God and if there is, what is He like? Is there anything after death and, if so, what is it? What – honestly – is the point of life? What's it all about?

You'll be a rare person if such questions have never entered your head! The human mind is endlessly inquisitive. We like questions – but we prefer answers.

Well, if we have never reached a satisfying conclusion about questions of this nature, perhaps what we need is the kind of time and space which retirement can offer us to think seriously about some of them. There are people and books which will provide resources for our searching, but much of it really involves space to think. Often a quiet weekend away will offer more clues to the troubled mind or the questioning spirit than any number of clever books. However, books can help. You would be surprised (if you haven't tried them) what treasures can be found in books about history, art, travel and science. And that's not to mention the treasures of the Bible!

> **The 'God-question' is one that has fascinated people since the dawn of time.**
>
> MEMO

IS THERE A GOD?

The 'God-question' is one that has fascinated people since the dawn of time. It's interesting that the vast majority of human beings all through history, including today, have decided that there is a God, or a Supreme Being or Power that oversees the creation and its creatures. Even in our very scientific and sceptical culture, the great majority of people – including both intellectuals and what we might call 'ordinary' men and women – believe in a 'God' of some sort.

In one way that's surprising, because it is of course quite impossible to prove the existence of God, just as it's equally impossible to disprove it. Most people may believe in a 'God' or a creative 'force' because they can't accept the idea that our existence can be explained by random choice or accident. But many have at some time or another had an experience which has convinced them of the reality of a spiritual dimension to life, and some are quite sure that they have encountered God. That encounter – whatever may have led to it – can open up further discoveries. The God who has touched our lives is the Father of Jesus, whom Christians worship as the Saviour of the world, the One who described Himself as the 'way' to the Father Himself (John 14:6). That in turn leads to the possibility of a whole new relationship with God, one in which we can experience Him in daily life, know forgiveness and an inner peace of mind, the irresistible sense that we are loved and valued. Faith of that kind is a personal choice, of course, but to go through life and not even investigate the 'God' issue seems to be tantamount to wilful neglect.

Life after death

Life after death becomes (as we have seen earlier) an important, or perhaps I should say more pressing, question as we enter our later years. Surprisingly, perhaps, in this atheistic age, in my experience I have found that most people believe (even if in a vague kind of way) that there is something after death. In years and years of talking to bereaved people, I have never met one who believed that the person they mourned had 'ceased to exist'. It just doesn't 'feel' like it.

That's not a knock-down case for life after death, of course. Christians would want to argue it from the resurrection of Jesus from the dead, and others cite various experiences they have had following the death of someone near to them. Many people 'feel' rather than 'believe' that there is life beyond death. Some would argue that although it seems such an unlikely idea, it is remarkable that the vast majority of human beings down the ages have believed in it.

Again, it's a question of personal decision, but there can hardly be a more relevant issue to consider for those of us approaching the point at which we shall find out the answer soon enough, one way or the other!

What's life *for*?

Simply to ask the question is to beg the answer, because to say life is 'for' something is to assume that it has a purpose, and some people would deny that there is any purpose to life beyond living it. We are part of the evolutionary process, they would say, and at the end will simply bequeath our genes, and perhaps a little bit of wisdom, to those who follow after us.

However, there's no doubt most people do think that life has a purpose, though they may differ widely over what they think it is. From a religious point of view the purpose of life, as the Westminster Shorter Catechism says, is 'to glorify God and enjoy Him forever'. Life is a garden of spiritual discovery, and the prize is the knowledge of a loving Creator. Many people would see this as a very beautiful and positive view of life, and certainly as we get older and our experiences of life multiply, we may well reckon that it doesn't seem like a lonely and meaningless journey to nowhere.

At any rate, the years of retirement could well prove a rewarding testing ground for ideas and thoughts like these. We could find someone – a Christian friend, a wise pastor, a relative who seems to have advanced a bit further along this road than we have – and talk it through in an unhurried and open way.

Whatever our own beliefs now, or in the future, it must surely be true that life is made better by a sense of purpose. In our later years we may well hope to see the fruit of that purpose in the lives that we have influenced – those we have loved, those we have tried to teach and encourage, and those with whom we have shared wonderful experiences of beauty, love and truth.

At the end of the journey, the most rewarding thing is to know that the lives we have touched have been the better for the experience, and that the lives that have touched ours have received our gratitude and love.

Next, a little fantasy for those facing retirement very soon – a dream, or is it a nightmare?

Retirement starts next Monday

It's been years in the waiting, but I've checked in the diary and my retirement date is this Friday, which means next Monday is the first day of the rest of my life. I also see that I've got a leaving 'do' on Friday. No idea what that might involve, except that I think the boss is going to come and 'say a few words'.

My friends in the drawing office will be there, of course, which means there'll be plenty of laughs. Probably they'll have planned some massive and embarrassing leg-pull, but I'm used to their tricks and will spot it a mile off. We'll have a few drinks, I imagine, hug each other (might get to kiss one or two of them, as well). Then I'll empty my desk (management was very precise about that, bless her), take my coat off the hook for the last time, and go home.

MEMO ... 'the best is yet to be' ...

It will be funny, really, catching the bus for the very last time from the office, walking up the road, putting the key in the door, and thinking, 'I won't be doing that again'. What I can't decide at the moment is whether I'm pleased, confused or unhappy at the prospect of the end of my working life.

I'm certainly pleased not to have to get up on cold mornings and wait at the stop for a bus that sometimes doesn't come. And I'm pleased (with a few reservations) about the prospect of spending more time at home with my wife, Louise. The reservations aren't because we've got 'problems', or anything like that, but that I shall feel I'm invading her 'territory' and putting our thirty-two years of marriage to the ultimate test of twenty-four/seven contact. We love each other, no doubt about that, but you know they say 'absence makes the heart grow fonder'? If that's true, does 'presence make the heart grow colder'? I hope not.

Then I'm rather confused as to what I'm going to do with myself during all that extra time I'm going to have. Did somebody say sixty hours a week extra? Being 'busy-busy' has been my lifestyle, and I'm a bit worried I'll go mad looking at the walls or reading and rereading the newspaper. Yes, of course I'll take on a few things – new hobbies, perhaps some study or a course or two … My friend Geoff even said he'd teach me to play golf! But it does seem a bit unsettling when you don't know what's going to fill up all those spare days.

Unhappy? No, I don't think I am, and I don't see why I should be. I've worked, man and boy (as they say), for forty-two years, and I think I've earned a break. Louise says that 'the best is yet to be' and she's generally right about this kind of thing. I certainly hope so.

Ah well, time to finish today's work. Just four days to go. And then, well, the rest of my life – or the life of rest? I suppose that's up to me.

The Ten Commandments (Final Version)

1 BE POSITIVE: Remember, this is a junction, not the terminus. Life will be a bit different, but you are still you and the people who really matter to you still matter. Don't get drawn into self-pity or pointless regret for the past. Think of all you can do *now*.

2 RELAX: Take your foot off the gas. There's no need now to live life in the fast lane. There's time to do things, to think, to make plans. Don't rush it! Space and time are gifts of God – use them!

3 DO SOMETHING NEW: A new hobby or pastime. A new friend or friends. A new interest. A new haircut or dress-style. A new look for the garden. You are not *past it*!

4 OPEN YOUR EYES: See things you hadn't noticed while you were working – sunrise and sunset; country villages; trees and leaves; old churches; the stars at night; the city roofs by moonlight.

5 KEEP YOUR BRAIN WORKING: Visit the library. Learn to use the Internet. Join the U3A. Enrol in a reading group. Walk and talk with a companion. Do a course at the local College of Further Education. Try a different daily paper!

6 GET INVOLVED: You've still got a lot to offer, so *offer* it! Volunteer to help in the local charity shop. Agree to be a school governor, club secretary, treasurer, press officer or chair. Get active in local politics or the church. Explore opportunities for mission, travel, working with (or spending time with) younger people.

7 VALUE THOSE YOU LOVE: They will mean more to you now than ever before, so cherish them. Strengthen your existing relationships and nurture new ones. Make time for people – they matter more than things.

8 WATCH YOUR HEALTH: Without getting obsessed, keep an eye on things such as regular exercise, diet (not too many ready meals, chips or cheese!), rest and relaxation. Take up a sport, walk more, join a gym. Have your eyes tested, get the GP to check your cholesterol from time to time, turn up for the autumn flu jab.

9 USE THE GIFT OF TIME: All through our working life our time has been largely shaped by our employment. Now, it is ours – or, rather, it is God's personal gift to us. Responsibly and reverently, consider how that precious gift should be used.

10 LEARN TO LIVE WITH YOURSELF: Try to practise a bit of solitude. It's surprising how satisfying a day spent apparently doing nothing can be if we treat it as an opportunity to think, reflect, pray, meditate and be comfortably at home with who we are.

National Distributors

UK: (and countries not listed below)
CWR, Waverley Abbey House, Waverley Lane, Farnham, Surrey GU9 8EP.
Tel: (01252) 784700 Outside UK (44) 1252 784700 Email: mail@cwr.org.uk

AUSTRALIA: KI Entertainment, Unit 21 317-321 Woodpark Road,
Smithfield, New South Wales 2164. Tel: 1 800 850 777
Fax: 02 9604 3699 Email: sales@kientertainment.com.au

CANADA: David C Cook Distribution Canada, PO Box 98, 55 Woodslee
Avenue, Paris, Ontario N3L 3E5. Tel: 1800 263 2664
Email: sandi.swanson@davidccook.ca

GHANA: Challenge Enterprises of Ghana, PO Box 5723, Accra.
Tel: (021) 222437/223249 Fax: (021) 226227 Email: ceg@africaonline.com.gh

HONG KONG: Cross Communications Ltd, 1/F, 562A Nathan Road, Kowloon.
Tel: 2780 1188 Fax: 2770 6229 Email: cross@crosshk.com

INDIA: Crystal Communications, 10-3-18/4/1, East Marredpalli, Secunderabad
– 500026, Andhra Pradesh. Tel/Fax: (040) 27737145
Email: crystal_edwj@rediffmail.com

KENYA: Keswick Books and Gifts Ltd, PO Box 10242-00400, Nairobi.
Tel: (020) 2226047/312639 Email: sales.keswick@africaonline.co.ke

MALAYSIA: Canaanland, No. 25 Jalan PJU 1A/41B, NZX Commercial Centre,
Ara Jaya, 47301 Petaling Jaya, Selangor. Tel: (03) 7885 0540/1/2
Fax: (03) 7885 0545 Email: info@canaanland.com.my

Salvation Publishing and Distribution Sdn Bhd, 23 Jalan SS 2/64,
47300 Petaling Jaya, Selangor. Tel: (03) 78766411/78766797
Fax: (03) 78757066/78756360 Email: info@salvationbookcentre.com

NEW ZEALAND: KI Entertainment, Unit 21 317-321 Woodpark Road,
Smithfield, New South Wales 2164, Australia. Tel: 0 800 850 777
Fax: +612 9604 3699 Email: sales@kientertainment.com.au

NIGERIA: FBFM, Helen Baugh House, 96 St Finbarr's College Road, Akoka,
Lagos. Tel: (01) 7747429/4700218/825775/827264 Email: fbfm_1@yahoo.com

PHILIPPINES: OMF Literature Inc, 776 Boni Avenue, Mandaluyong City.
Tel: (02) 531 2183 Fax: (02) 531 1960 Email: gloadlaon@omflit.com

SINGAPORE: Alby Commercial Enterprises Pte Ltd, 95 Kallang Avenue
#04-00, AIS Industrial Building, 339420. Tel: (65) 629 27238
Fax: (65) 629 27235 Email: marketing@alby.com.sg

SOUTH AFRICA: Struik Christian Books, 80 MacKenzie Street, PO Box 1144,
Cape Town 8000. Tel: (021) 462 4360 Fax: (021) 461 3612
Email: info@struikchristianmedia.co.za

SRI LANKA: Christombu Publications (Pvt) Ltd, Bartleet House,
65 Braybrooke Place, Colombo 2. Tel: (9411) 2421073/2447665
Email: dhanad@bartleet.com

USA: David C Cook Distribution Canada, PO Box 98, 55 Woodslee Avenue,
Paris, Ontario N3L 3E5, Canada. Tel: 1800 263 2664
Email: sandi.swanson@davidccook.ca

CWR is a Registered Charity – Number 294387
CWR is a Limited Company registered in England –
Registration Number 1990308

Courses and seminars

Publishing and new media

Conference facilities

Transforming lives

CWR's vision is to enable people to experience personal transformation through applying God's Word to their lives and relationships.

Our Bible-based training and resources help people around the world to:
- Grow in their walk with God
- Understand and apply Scripture to their lives
- Resource themselves and their church
- Develop pastoral care and counselling skills
- Train for leadership
- Strengthen relationships, marriage and family life

and much more.

Our insightful writers provide daily Bible-reading notes and other resources for all ages, and our experienced course designers and presenters have gained an international reputation for excellence and effectiveness.

CWR's Training and Conference Centre in Surrey, England, provides excellent facilities in an idyllic setting – ideal for both learning and spiritual refreshment.

CWR, Waverley Abbey House, Waverley Lane, Farnham, Surrey GU9 8EP, UK

Telephone:
+44 (0)1252 784700
Email:
info@cwr.org.uk
Website:
www.cwr.org.uk

Registered Charity No 294387
Company Registration No 1990308

Many people think the Bible is ...

BORING*

*But CWR daily devotionals are changing that.

Our range of daily Bible-reading notes has something for everyone – and to engage with even the most demanding members of the family!

Whether you want themed devotional writing, life-application notes, a deeper Bible study or meditations tailored to women or the growing minds of children and young people, we have just the one for you.

To order or for more information, including current prices, visit **www.cwr.org.uk/store** or any Christian bookshop.

CWR'S DAILY BIBLE-READING NOTES

THEMED
DEVOTIONAL

FOR WOMEN

LIFE
APPLICATION

DEEPER
BIBLE STUDY

FOR 14-18s

FOR 11-15s

FOR 7-11s

FOR 3-6s

Learn profound truths from simple stories

This charming book of 52 modern-day parables, personal stories and reflections will take you into the heart of someone very special who has lived through two world wars, and you will enjoy a glimpse into the secret history of her heartaches and joys.

Short, simple prayers at the end of some of the stories will move you closer to the God who loves us faithfully.

As Time Goes By
by Marie Kane-Dudley
148-page hardback, 147x187mm
ISBN: 978-1-85345-487-5